I0454951

FREEDOM OF EXPRESSION

EXCERPTED

FROM THE

2011 ANNUAL REPORT

OF THE

CONGRESSIONAL-EXECUTIVE
COMMISSION ON CHINA

ONE HUNDRED TWELFTH CONGRESS

FIRST SESSION

OCTOBER 10, 2011

Printed for the use of the Congressional-Executive Commission on China

Available via the World Wide Web: http://www.cecc.gov

U.S. GOVERNMENT PRINTING OFFICE

70–938 PDF   WASHINGTON : 2011

For sale by the Superintendent of Documents, U.S. Government Printing Office
Internet: bookstore.gpo.gov   Phone: toll free (866) 512–1800; DC area (202) 512–1800
Fax: (202) 512–2104   Mail: Stop IDCC, Washington, DC 20402–0001

CONGRESSIONAL-EXECUTIVE COMMISSION ON CHINA

LEGISLATIVE BRANCH COMMISSIONERS

House

CHRISTOPHER H. SMITH, New Jersey,
Chairman

Senate

SHERROD BROWN, Ohio, *Cochairman*
MAX BAUCUS, Montana
CARL LEVIN, Michigan
DIANNE FEINSTEIN, California
JEFF MERKLEY, Oregon
SUSAN COLLINS, Maine
JAMES RISCH, Idaho

EXECUTIVE BRANCH COMMISSIONERS

SETH D. HARRIS, Department of Labor
MARIA OTERO, Department of State
FRANCISCO J. SÁNCHEZ, Department of Commerce
KURT M. CAMPBELL, Department of State
NISHA DESAI BISWAL, U.S. Agency for International Development

PAUL B. PROTIC, *Staff Director*
LAWRENCE T. LIU, *Deputy Staff Director*

(II)

FREEDOM OF EXPRESSION

Findings

- During the Commission's 2011 reporting year, Chinese officials continued to maintain a broad range of restrictions on free expression that do not comply with international human rights standards, including Article 19 of the International Covenant on Civil and Political Rights and Articles 19 and 29 of the Universal Declaration of Human Rights. While such standards permit states in limited circumstances to restrict expression to protect interests such as national security and public order, Chinese restrictions covered a much broader range of activity, including expression critical of the Communist Party and peaceful dissent. Despite this, Chinese officials continue to point to Internet development in China as proof of freedom of expression and to argue that Chinese restrictions comply with international law, including in the case of imprisoned Nobel Peace Prize winner Liu Xiaobo.
- This past year was marked by a major crackdown on Internet and press freedom that exemplified the range of tools officials can use to restrict the free flow of information. The crackdown began in mid-February following protests in the Middle East and North Africa and the appearance of online calls for "Jasmine" protests in China.
- While international and domestic observers continued to note the vibrancy of Internet and cell phone use in China, government and Party officials showed little sign of loosening political control. Top leaders, including President Hu Jintao, called for "strengthening" the Party's guidance of online public opinion, as well as the Party's leadership over the Internet. Officials established a central-level agency to tighten supervision of the Internet and issued regulations to increase monitoring of Internet use in public places. Censors continued to block the sharing of online information that officials deemed to be politically sensitive, including news of the Nobel Peace Prize award to imprisoned intellectual and reform advocate Liu Xiaobo, the calls for "Jasmine" protests, and words such as "human rights" and "democracy." At times, citizen expression on China's microblogs overwhelmed censors, including following the Wenzhou high-speed train accident in July 2011.
- Officials insisted that any reform of the media industry would result in "no change in the Party's control over the media." Officials continued to issue broad guidance, such as telling the media it was their "common responsibility" to promote the 90th anniversary of the Party's founding. Officials also continued to issue specific directives, such as how to cover the protests in the Middle East and North Africa and the

award of the Nobel Peace Prize to Liu Xiaobo. Harassment of foreign journalists reached a new height this past year, including beatings and threats of expulsion of journalists who attempted to report on the "Jasmine" protest strolls.

• Officials continued to arbitrarily restrict expression by abusing vague criminal law provisions and abusing broad regulations and registration requirements applicable to journalists, publishers, news media, and the Internet. Citizens who criticized the government were charged with national security crimes such as "subversion." Official campaigns to train and supervise journalists conducted in the name of combating corruption continued to be heavily imbued with political indoctrination. Officials continued to use campaigns they described as intended to enforce the law to instead target "illegal" political and religious publications. Such publications included ones that "defame the Party and state leaders" or "contain political rumors that create ideological confusion."

Recommendations

Members of the U.S. Congress and Administration officials are encouraged to:

○ Raise concerns over and draw enhanced international attention to the Chinese government's continued insistence that its restrictions on freedom of expression are consistent with international standards. Chinese officials assert that such measures are taken to protect national security or public order when available information indicates that many measures are aimed at silencing opposition to the Party or blocking the free flow of information on politically sensitive topics. Emphasize that the Chinese government's position undermines international human rights standards for free expression, particularly those contained in Article 19 of the International Covenant on Civil and Political Rights and Articles 19 and 29 of the Universal Declaration of Human Rights. Emphasize to Chinese officials that Communist Party and government censorship of the Internet and the press can lead to instability by eroding public faith in the media and government.

○ Engage in dialogue and exchanges with Chinese officials on the issue of how governments can best ensure that restrictions on freedom of expression are not abused and do not exceed the scope necessary to protect national security, minors, and public order. Emphasize the importance of procedural protections such as public participation in formulation of restrictions on free expression, transparency regarding implementation of such restrictions, and independent review of such restrictions. Reiterate Chinese officials' own calls for greater transparency and public participation in lawmaking. Such discussions may be part of a broader discussion on how both the U.S. and Chinese governments can work together to ensure the protection of common interests on the Internet, including protecting minors, computer security, and privacy.

○ Acknowledge the Chinese government's efforts to expand access to the Internet and cell phones, especially in rural areas, while continuing to press officials to comply with international standards. Support the research and development of technologies that enable Chinese citizens to access and share political and religious content that they are entitled to access and share under international human rights standards. Support practices and Chinese-language tools and training materials that enable Chinese citizens to access and share content in a way that ensures their security and privacy. Support the dissemination of online Chinese-language information on the Internet, especially popular Chinese social media sites, that discusses the rights and freedoms to which Chinese citizens are entitled under international standards.

○ Raise concerns regarding Chinese officials' instrumental use of the law, including vague national security charges, as a tool to suppress citizens' rights to freedom of expression, and question whether such actions are in keeping with the spirit of the "rule of law."

○ Elevate concern over the increased harassment of foreign journalists, who this past year have been beaten and threatened with expulsion for attempting to report on events of public concern. Emphasize that such treatment is not in keeping with regulations issued for the 2008 Beijing Summer Olympic Games in which Chinese officials promised greater freedoms for foreign journalists, and is not in keeping with the treatment Chinese journalists are afforded when reporting on events in the United States.

○ Call for the release of Liu Xiaobo and other political prisoners imprisoned for allegedly committing crimes of endangering state security and other crimes but whose only offense was to peacefully express support for political reform or criticism of government policies, including Tan Zuoren (sentenced in February 2010 to five years in prison after using the Internet to organize an independent investigation into school collapses in an earthquake).

Introduction

During the Commission's 2011 reporting year, Chinese officials maintained a broad range of restrictions on free expression that do not comply with international human rights standards. While such standards permit states in limited circumstances to restrict expression to protect interests such as national security and public order, Chinese restrictions covered a much broader range of activity, including peaceful expression critical of the Communist Party. Chinese officials showed little sign of loosening political control over the Internet and cell phones. They called for strengthening the Party's guidance of online opinion and censored politically sensitive information, including searches for "human rights" or "democracy." At times, citizen expression on China's popular microblogs overwhelmed censors, including following a high-speed train accident in July. A top official said there would be "no change in the Party's control over the media," amidst censorship of events such as the Nobel Peace Prize award to imprisoned Chinese intellectual and reform advocate Liu Xiaobo and intensified harassment of foreign journalists. Officials continued to abuse vague criminal charges, including subversion, to target peaceful speech critical of the Party. Officials maintained broad regulations and registration requirements applicable to journalists, publishers, news media, and the Internet.

International Standards for Free Expression

Many Chinese restrictions on free expression do not comply with international human rights standards. Article 19 of the International Covenant on Civil and Political Rights (ICCPR) and Articles 19 and 29 of the Universal Declaration of Human Rights permit officials to restrict expression so long as it is (1) for the purpose of respecting the rights or reputations of others or protecting national security, public order, public health or morals, or the general welfare; (2) set forth in law; and (3) necessary and the least restrictive means to achieve the purported aim.[1] Regarding the purpose requirement, the UN Human Rights Council has said restrictions on "discussion of government policies and political debate," "peaceful demonstrations or political activities, including for peace and democracy," and "expression of dissent," are inconsistent with Article 19 of the ICCPR.[2] As outlined in this section, Chinese officials continued to restrict expression on the Internet and in the media for impermissible purposes, such as to stifle peaceful criticism of the Communist Party. As to restrictions clearly set forth in law, Chinese officials this past year abused vaguely worded criminal law provisions and resorted to extralegal measures to arbitrarily restrict free expression. As to the narrowness requirement, as documented in this section, Chinese restrictions continued to be overly broad and disproportionate to protecting the stated interest. In May 2011, the UN Special Rapporteur on the Promotion and Protection of the Right to Freedom of Opinion and Expression noted that restrictions on expression should be applied by an independent body and include the possibility of remedy against abuse.[3] As noted in this section, in China there remained no independent checks on government abuse.

Official Response to Overseas Protests and Calls for Domestic "Jasmine" Protests

This past year was marked by a crackdown on free expression in China in early 2011 that followed protests in the Middle East and North Africa and the appearance of online calls for "Jasmine" protests domestically. Protests in the Middle East began in Tunisia in December 2010 and soon spread to Egypt, Libya, and other countries in the region. In February 2011, the "Jasmine" calls began circulating online in China.[4] They called for weekly non-violent protest strolls in select cities to demand an end to corruption and to promote issues such as judicial independence, free expression, and political reform.[5]

MEDIA AND INTERNET CENSORSHIP

Officials reportedly censored Chinese media coverage of the Middle East and North Africa protests. According to leaked censorship instructions, officials allegedly ordered Chinese media to use only stories issued by the central government news agency, Xinhua, and banned reporting on demands for democracy in the Middle East or drawing comparisons to China's political system.[6] Western media observed Chinese media relying heavily on Xinhua stories and observed one-sided coverage emphasizing the dangers of democracy for countries not ready for it.[7] At the time, online censors reportedly blocked searches of the words "Egypt," "Libya," "Jasmine," and "democracy."[8] The duration and effectiveness of the censorship was unclear. Foreign media attempting to report on the "Jasmine" protests encountered intense harassment. [See Foreign Journalists below for more information.]

HARASSMENT, DETENTIONS OF CHINESE CITIZENS

Starting in mid-February 2011, Chinese authorities also targeted large numbers of writers, artists, Internet bloggers, lawyers, and reform advocates. Many were outspoken critics of the government; some tried to share information about the "Jasmine" protest calls, while the connection of others, if any, to the calls was unclear.[9] Officials detained numerous citizens on national security and public disturbance charges.[10] [For information on these and other individual cases in the crackdown, see Internet and Other Electronic Media, and Abuse of Criminal Laws To Punish Free Expression in this section.] The UN Working Group on Enforced or Involuntary Disappearances and other international groups noted reports of numerous Chinese citizens having gone missing or disappearing into official custody with little or no information about their charges or whereabouts.[11] [For more information on the apparent disregard of criminal procedural protections in connection with the disappearances, see Enforced Disappearances in Section II—Criminal Justice.]

Internet and Other Electronic Media

BLOCKING AND FILTERING POLITICAL CONTENT

In China, officials are not transparent about the content that is blocked or why it is blocked,[12] and they continue to arbitrarily block content for purposes impermissible under international standards. Chinese authorities expressed anger over the awarding of the Nobel Peace Prize to imprisoned prominent intellectual and reform advocate Liu Xiaobo in October 2010, for example, and blocked online searches for "Nobel Peace Prize" or "Liu Xiaobo" and text messages containing Liu's name.[13] In January 2011, authorities reportedly banned hundreds of words, including "democracy" and "human rights" from cell phone text messages.[14] Politically sensitive Web sites continued to be blocked, including a popular Tibetan culture site, an anticorruption site, and a public health advocacy Web site.[15] Officials also continued to block information in a disproportionate manner that did not appear necessary to achieve a legitimate aim. For example, access to overseas sites such as Facebook, Twitter, and YouTube remained completely blocked.[16] In late May 2011, officials reportedly imposed broad blocks on Internet and cell phone access in the northern part of the Inner Mongolia Autonomous Region following a series of mostly peaceful protests sparked by the death of a herder.[17]

Officials continued to detain and harass Chinese citizens who sought to share politically sensitive content online. In each case, the activity appeared to pose little threat to national security or public order, or the punishment appeared disproportionate to the alleged offense. For example, rights defender Cheng Jianping (who uses the pseudonym Wang Yi) sent a satirical Twitter message urging anti-Japanese protesters to converge on the Japanese pavilion at the Shanghai 2010 World Expo.[18] The Xinxiang City Reeducation Through Labor (RTL) Committee in Henan province ordered her to serve one year of RTL in November 2010.[19] In April 2011, authorities in Chongqing municipality ordered a citizen to serve RTL for posting scatological humor in a critique of the policies of Chongqing's Party Secretary Bo Xilai.[20] In November 2010, Shanghai police interrogated the writer Xia Shang after he offered to buy flowers for victims of a Shanghai fire in an Internet post.[21] Officials treated citizens who sought to share information about the calls for domestic "Jasmine" protests, which appeared to be a nonviolent call for political reform, as threats to the state. The detained included Hua Chunhui, an insurance company manager and activist who reportedly sent Twitter messages about the "Jasmine" protest calls and was charged with endangering state security.[22] In April 2011, officials in Jiangsu province ordered Hua to serve 18 months of RTL.[23] In February, police in Harbin city, Heilongjiang province, detained Internet blogger Liang Haiyi on suspicion of the crime of "subversion of state power." Police accused her of posting information about the "Jasmine" protests on the popular QQ microblogging site.[24]

The types of content prohibited online in China are not clearly defined in law, and thus conflict with international standards. Chinese Internet regulations contain vague and broad prohibitions on content that, for example, "harms the honor or interests of the nation," "spreads rumors," or "disrupts national policies on religion."[25] Chinese law does not define these concepts.[26] In China, the government places the burden on Internet service and content providers to monitor and remove content based on these vague standards and to maintain records of such activity and report it to the government.[27] In February 2011, a manager at Renren, a major social media company similar to Facebook, said that the company censored sensitive content using a staff of 500 and a keyword filtering system, and that the "CEO would have to have a coffee with the government" for any misstep.[28] The Party's influence over the technology sector was evident in June, when more than 60 representatives from top Chinese Internet companies, including Sina and Baidu, gathered in Shanghai to commemorate the Party's 90th anniversary.[29] Also in June, Sina announced plans to launch an English microblog site in the United States, which could have the effect of exporting Chinese censorship to overseas markets.[30] The U.S.-based company Google, which has operations in China and which in early 2010 challenged Chinese censorship requirements, reportedly continued to face problems in China. In March 2011, Google reported that the Chinese government appeared to be interfering with its email service in China and making it look like a technical problem.[31] The government denied the charge.[32] In June, Google reported that an attack on hundreds of personal Gmail accounts, including those of Chinese political activists, senior U.S. officials, and journalists, had originated from China.[33] The Party's official newspaper rejected the allegation.[34]

PRIOR RESTRAINTS ON THE INTERNET

In addition to blocking certain types of content, officials in China control the Internet by determining who gains access to the medium through numerous licensing requirements (i.e., prior restraints). All Web sites hosted in China are required either to be licensed by or registered with the government, and sites providing news content or audio and video services require an additional license or registration.[35] In a 2011 report, the UN Special Rapporteur for Free Expression said that licensing requirements "cannot be justified in the case of the Internet, as it can accommodate an unlimited number of points of entry and an essentially unlimited number of users."[36] In October 2010, Chinese media reported that as of the end of September 2010 Chinese Internet companies had inspected nearly 1.8 million Web sites and shut down 3,000 for failing to register.[37] In July 2011, the Chinese Academy of Social Sciences (CASS) reported a 41 percent decrease in the number of Web sites in China in 2010 to 1.91 million sites.[38] The report's editor cited government campaigns targeting "obscene" sites and the economic downturn as reasons for the decrease, and said in recent years few sites had been closed "purely to control speech."[39] Other observers in China, however, attributed the decrease to the chilling effect of expanding government control.[40] The CASS study also claimed that the United States was using new media, including the Voice of America, to threaten China's "ideological safety."[41]

EXPANDING OVERALL ACCESS, WHILE MAINTAINING CONTROL

The government has pledged to expand access to the Internet and cell phones.[42] Official statistics indicate that by the end of 2010, there were 457 million Internet users in China, including a growing number in rural areas, and by April 2011, 900 million mobile phone accounts.[43] Officials have sought to expand the Internet to promote economic development and government propaganda.[44] Still, international observers and Western media continue to note the difficulties officials have in controlling this emerging and vibrant space for expression, including expression of criticism of the government and discussion of some politically sensitive topics.[45] In July 2011, for example, users on China's two most popular Twitter-type microblogs posted some 26 million messages after a high-speed train crash near Wenzhou city, Zhejiang province.[46] Officials reportedly censored some messages, but a large number of messages either were allowed through or appeared too quickly for censors to react.[47]

Official statements and actions continue to emphasize control rather than freedom on the Internet. The importance of maintaining official control was reinforced in May 2011, when officials established a State Internet Information Office to "supervise and urge relevant departments to strengthen their supervision of online content, and to be responsible for approvals for online news services and other related services as well as day-to-day oversight."[48] In China, the Communist Party exercises tight control over government agencies that manage the media and Internet.[49] This relationship gives the Party discretion to use government restrictions not just for the purpose of regulating pornography, intellectual property violations, and protecting minors—permissible purposes under international standards—but also to serve the Party's interests. In February 2011, President Hu Jintao called for "strengthening the mechanisms for guiding online public opinion."[50] The practice of authorities paying Chinese citizens to post comments favorable to the government and Party on the Internet reportedly continued.[51] In February, Communist Party Politburo Standing Committee member Zhou Yongkang said authorities should "coalesce a comprehensive" structure for managing the Internet "under the Party committee's unified leadership."[52] In Beijing, authorities reportedly issued regulations requiring bars, hotels, and other public places to purchase and install costly software to monitor the identities of people using wireless services at those locations.[53]

Abuse of Criminal Law To Punish Free Expression

Officials continued to use the criminal charges of "subversion" and "inciting subversion" (Article 105 of the PRC Criminal Law) this past year, in part in connection with the crackdown that followed protests in the Middle East and North Africa and the calls for "Jasmine" protests domestically.[54] According to the non-governmental organization (NGO) Chinese Human Rights Defenders, out of a total of 48 individuals detained since mid-February 2011, officials had charged at least 17 with "subversion" or "inciting subversion."[55] Ran Yunfei, a prolific writer, blogger, and activist, was arrested in March for "inciting subversion."[56] Authorities released him in August but placed him under "residential restriction" for six months, restricting his movements and ability to write and speak.[57] In March, police in Ningbo city, Zhejiang province, detained prominent blogger Guo Weidong on suspicion of "inciting subversion of state power" after alleging he had forwarded information online about the protests.[58]

Officials also charged numerous persons with "creating disturbances," a crime under Article 293 of the PRC Criminal Law.[59] Officials detained the human rights activist Wei Qiang on the charge of "creating a disturbance" in March 2011, before releasing him on bail to await trial in April.[60] In February, Wei was at the site of one of the "Jasmine" protest strolls in Beijing and reported on the scene using his Twitter account. Amid the broader crackdown, authorities in March 2011 also detained the Beijing-based rights advocate Wang Lihong on the charge of creating a disturbance, but in connection with activities stemming from almost a year earlier.[61] They alleged that Wang had used the Internet to organize protests outside a court in support of three bloggers accused of defamation for helping a woman call on officials to reinvestigate her daughter's death.[62] In September, after a trial reportedly marked by procedural irregularities,[63] a Beijing court sentenced Wang to nine months in prison for creating a disturbance.[64]

In the case of the well-known artist Ai Weiwei, officials charged him with economic crimes, alleging that his company had evaded "a huge amount of tax."[65] Ai had become an outspoken critic of government policies and had been keeping track of the lawyers, bloggers, and activists swept up in the crackdown, when officials detained him in April.[66] Authorities had refused to notify his family of the charges against him or his whereabouts and kept him at a secret location, purportedly under "residential surveillance."[67] During his 81 days in custody, Ai was reportedly kept in a cell without windows and was accompanied by two guards.[68] Authorities released Ai on bail in June on the condition that he not give interviews or use Twitter.[69] In August, Ai resumed his Twitter messages and told a Western newspaper, "I can't be alive and not express my feelings."[70]

The actual threat these citizens posed to state security and public order or whether the underlying crime was the actual motivation for official action is unclear, as details regarding many of these cases remain limited. Available information suggests that officials targeted the citizens to stifle political expression and dissent. Many of the citizens targeted had track records of criticizing the government and Communist Party and advocating for democracy and human rights.[71] As the UN Working Group on Arbitrary Detention and Chinese Human Rights Defenders have noted in recent years, the vagueness of Chinese crimes of endangering state security, including subversion, lends itself to official abuse of freedom of speech, and Chinese courts make little assessment of whether the speech in question poses a threat to state security.[72] There were other cases of alleged subversion or splittism this past year. In October 2010, officials in Wuhan city, Hubei province, arrested the prolific blogger Li Tie on charges of subversion; Li had written numerous essays in support of democracy.[73] In November, Beijing authorities detained activist Bai Dongping on inciting subversion charges after he posted online a photo of the 1989 Tiananmen protests.[74] In December, three Tibetan writers, Kalsang Jinpa, Jangtse Donkho, and Buddha were sentenced to prison terms of three to four years for inciting splittism after articles they had written about the 2008 Tibetan protests appeared in a magazine.[75] In March 2011, authorities in Suining city, Sichuan province, sentenced democracy advocate Liu Xianbin to 10 years in prison for seeking to incite subversion by writing essays advocating for, among other things, democracy, and posting them on Web sites outside of China.[76]

Authorities Defend Liu Xiaobo Case on Grounds of International Law

After imprisoned prominent intellectual and reform advocate Liu Xiaobo was awarded the Nobel Peace Prize in October 2010, Chinese authorities sought to defend their handling of his case as consistent with international law. After the award was announced, China's central government news agency, Xinhua, issued an analysis of the case based on the findings of a Chinese criminal law scholar, Gao Mingxuan.[77] The analysis noted that international treaties and nearly every country's laws criminalize some speech, and that Liu's speech had sought to incite the overthrow of the Chinese government.[78] Xinhua failed to note that the essays and activities cited as evidence against Liu, who was sentenced to 11 years in prison, did not advocate violence and instead called for nonviolence and gradual political reform.[79] A May 2011 opinion of the UN Working Group on Arbitrary Detention concluded that Chinese authorities' handling of Liu's case violated both his right to fair trial and his right to political free speech as provided under international law.[80] Chinese officials responded to the Nobel announcement by detaining citizens who distributed leaflets and posted online messages in support of Liu.[81]

Extralegal Harassment

Chinese officials continued to physically harm, restrict the travel of, and otherwise extralegally harass citizens to punish and stifle expression. Under illegal home confinement after his release, self-trained legal advocate Chen Guangcheng and his wife Yuan Weijing recorded video of themselves describing the round-the-clock surveillance and harassment they faced.[82] After the video was smuggled out and posted online in February 2011, security officials reportedly beat Chen and Yuan on two occasions.[83] After the Nobel announcement in October 2010, authorities confined Liu Xia, the wife of Liu Xiaobo, to her home in Beijing and cut off her communications to the outside world.[84] A May 2011 opinion of the UN Working Group on Arbitrary Detention concluded that Liu Xia's house arrest violates international standards.[85] After his release from prison in December, China Democracy Party co-founder Qin Yongmin was harassed by police in Wuhan city, Hubei province, who accused him of speaking to reporters.[86] Officials refused to allow the noted writer Liao Yiwu to attend the March 2011 PEN World Writers Festival in New York and a literary festival in Australia in May.[87] In July, Liao escaped China at the Vietnam border. He fled to Berlin in anticipation of the publication of a memoir on the four years he spent in a Chinese prison for writing a poem on the 1989 Tiananmen protests.[88] The Buddhist leader Wu Zeheng reportedly has been beaten, harassed, and prevented from participating in a Buddhist celebration by authorities in Guangdong province following his release from prison in February 2010.[89] Wu previously served 11 years for alleged economic crimes, although reports connect that imprisonment to his issuance of letters to China's leadership calling for reforms and an end to corruption.[90]

Freedom of the Press

Chinese government and Communist Party control over the press continued to violate international standards. International experts identify media serving "as government mouthpieces instead of as independent bodies operating in the public interest" as a major challenge to free expression.[91] In China, officials expect the media to serve as the Party and government's mouthpiece. In a November 2010 speech on political reform, Liu Binjie, director of the government agency responsible for regulating the press, the General Administration on Press and Publication, said any reform must be "beneficial to strengthening and improving the Party's leadership over press and publishing work. . . . From beginning to end we must insist on . . . no change to the nature of press and publishing serving as mouthpiece of the Party and the people, no change in the Party's control over the media."[92] In January 2011, a spokesperson for the State Administration for Radio, Film, and Television (SARFT) said officials had ruled out any moves to commercialize radio and television stations. "Radio and television stations are the Party's important news media and battleground for propagandizing ideology and culture . . . and propaganda must remain its focus," he said.[93] In November 2010, the Party's official journal, Seeking Truth, cited the experience of the former Soviet Union to argue against any liberalization of China's press.[94]

Authorities have allowed reporters some room to exercise "public supervision" duties over local officials and local matters, but in recent years have sought to rein in this space. In the summer of 2010, for example, the Central Propaganda Department reportedly barred more commercially oriented "metropolitan" (*dushi*) newspapers from publishing "negative" stories about incidents in other geographic areas within China or carrying stories published by newspapers based in other areas, a practice known as "outside area supervision."[95] Rhetorically, officials continue to claim that the rights of legally recognized journalists should be protected, although the content of such rights remains unclear.[96] Emboldened by official claims that journalists deserve protection, Chinese journalists protested a series of incidents during the summer of 2010 in which local officials and commercial interests had targeted a number of journalists, including threatening them with charges of criminal defamation.[97] Despite such protests, a deputy editor at Caijing, a Chinese financial magazine known for its investigative reporting, noted the "core problem: our police and judiciary are not independent and there is widespread collusion between officials and enterprises."[98] In July, the Party issued an order censoring news coverage of a high-speed train accident in Wenzhou city, Zhejiang province, forcing newspapers to discard pages containing coverage of the incident.[99] The order came after Chinese citizens flooded the Internet with messages questioning officials' response and openness following the crash.[100] A number of Chinese journalists expressed outrage at the propaganda order on their blogs, and at least one news weekly appeared to ignore the order.[101]

POLITICAL CONTROL OF MEDIA THROUGH PARTY DIRECTIVES

This past year, officials continued to publicly issue broad directives on what China's domestic media should report, reminding journalists of their duty to "correctly" (*zhengque*) guide public opinion. On Journalists' Day in China in November 2010, Li Changchun, a member of the Standing Committee of the Political Bureau of the Communist Party Central Committee, said that "a correct public opinion orientation benefits the Party and the people."[102] He called on the news media to "propagandize the Party's positions."[103] To prepare for the 90th anniversary of the founding of the Chinese Communist Party in July 2011, Central Propaganda Department director Liu Yunshan said in April that covering the anniversary was the "common responsibility of media organizations at various levels."[104] He called on evening and metropolitan newspapers to "use vivid stories and inspiring topics to illustrate the glorious history of our Party's struggle" and urged online media to "help the large numbers of netizens understand the Party's great historical course by publishing special postings, background links, and online interviews."[105] In May 2011, an official at SARFT confirmed that television stations had been verbally ordered not to air detective and time travel shows during the anniversary period.[106]

The Party, through its Central Propaganda Department, lower level propaganda departments, and other government agencies, also issues more specific directives to the media on what they can and cannot report on. These directives are considered state secrets, but their contents continue to be leaked to the public and reported on by foreign and Hong Kong media and non-governmental organizations. In an April 2011 Washington Post story, unnamed Chinese editors and journalists confirmed the substance of a series of directives issued in March that appeared to reflect official nervousness over the North Africa and Middle East protests.[107] In January 2011, the International Federation of Journalists released a report documenting more than 80 censorship orders in 2010.[108] The orders reportedly blocked information on "public health, disasters, corruption and civil unrest."[109] A virtual news blackout, including the blacking out of Western stations broadcast in China, followed the Nobel Peace Prize announcement in October 2010.[110] The only news stories were from state-run media outlets such as Xinhua and Global Times, which reported on Chinese displeasure with the award.[111] In January 2011, the Central Propaganda Department reportedly ordered media not to use the phrase "civil society" in their reports.[112]

PUNISHMENT OF JOURNALISTS

Journalists and news media who issued news reports that authorities did not approve of continued to face punishment. In December 2010, a reporter at Southern Weekend said that the paper had been ordered to cease publication of an annual media award.[113] In January 2011, the outspoken journalist Chang Ping, who worked for the Southern Daily Group, reported that he had been dismissed from his job under pressure from authorities.[114] That same month, Time Weekly placed one of its editors, Peng Xiaoyun, on what appeared to be involuntary leave after the paper ran a story mentioning prominent activists and several signers of Charter 08.[115] Titled the "100 Most Influential People of Our Time" and published in mid-December, the list included Zhao Lianhai, the advocate for victims of tainted milk.[116] After the story's publication, copies reportedly were recalled and Peng and another editor were required to write self-criticisms.[117] In March 2011, Peng reported that she had been dismissed.[118] The publishers of another Guangzhou-based publication, South Wind Window, reportedly demoted its president and suspended another journalist after officials criticized a story they deemed "anti-government and anti-Communist Party."[119] Following the Wenzhou train crash, China's central television network suspended Wang Qinglei after the host of a program he produced questioned the Railway Ministry's response to the incident, and removed another program after it criticized the ministry's spokesman.[120]

POLITICAL CONTROL OF MEDIA THROUGH REGULATION OF EDITORS AND JOURNALISTS

All news media are subject to an extensive licensing system and continual government oversight. In order to legally report the news, domestic newspapers, magazines, and Web sites, as well as individual journalists, must obtain a license or accreditation from the government.[121] Radio and television broadcast journalists must pass a government-sponsored exam that tests them on basic knowledge of Marxist views of news and Communist Party principles.[122] In the 2010 Annual Report, the Commission reported that government officials were planning to require all journalists to pass a similar exam, but it is unclear whether this exam has been implemented.[123] Ongoing training initiatives for journalists continued to be heavily imbued with political indoctrination. In November, teleconferences with journalists across China were held in connection with a new campaign to "Stop False Reporting, Strengthen Social Responsibility, and Strengthen Construction of News Profession Ethics."[124] The campaign sought to "guide editors and journalists to grasp the basics of Marxist views of news . . . in order to strengthen the feeling of glory and mission in doing the Party's news work well."[125] According to an April 2011 article on the China Journalists Association Web site on 14 newspaper units that carried out "self-education," journalists at one Beijing newspaper were reminded that "news media are the mouthpiece of the Party and people . . . and not simply a commercial activity."[126]

International experts have criticized a general licensing requirement for journalists.[127] In a 2010 joint declaration on challenges to free expression, the UN Special Rapporteur on Freedom of Opinion and Expression and his international counterparts identified as challenges "registration requirements for print media" and government rules against "publishing false news."[128] Chinese officials continue to exercise their discretion to shut down unlicensed media. In March 2011, China's main press regulator, the General Administration on Press and Publication, announced a 100-day campaign to, among other objectives, shut down "illegal" reporting offices.[129]

FOREIGN JOURNALISTS

This past year the Commission observed a spike in the intensity and level of harassment against foreign journalists as they attempted to report on events considered sensitive by Chinese officials. In February 2011, foreign journalists who traveled to Linyi city, Shandong province, to report on the home confinement of self-trained legal advocate Chen Guangcheng encountered violent groups of men who roughed them up, threatened them with bricks, and destroyed equipment.[130] The journalists contacted local police but received no assistance.[131] In late February and early March 2011, Chinese authorities harassed foreign journalists attempting to cover the "Jasmine" protest strolls at sites in Beijing and other parts of China.[132] On February 27, reporters covering the Wangfujing site in Beijing met rough treatment from officials, and one journalist was reportedly beaten and later sought treatment at a hospital.[133] Chinese Foreign Minister Yang Jiechi denied that any foreign journalists had been beaten, and foreign ministry spokesperson Jiang Yu said the journalists had disrupted "normal order" and violated unspecified rules.[134] Harassment continued in the days that followed, with officials asking a journalist to sign a pledge promising never to report on the "Jasmine" protests and officials threatening to expel journalists or revoke their press credentials.[135] In April, plainclothes police detained, and in at least one case roughed up, foreign reporters attempting to cover an outdoor Christian religious gathering.[136] In May 2011, the professional association of international journalists in China, the Foreign Correspondents' Club of China, said 94 percent of survey respondents believed reporting conditions in China had deteriorated, with 70 percent saying they faced interference, violence, or other harassment during the past year, and 40 percent saying their sources had encountered official harassment.[137]

RESTRICTIONS ON "ILLEGAL" PUBLISHING AND POLITICAL AND RELIGIOUS PUBLICATIONS

The Chinese government continued to engage in campaigns to root out unlicensed publications and publications containing what officials deemed to be "illegal" political and religious content. In China, no one may publish, print, copy, or distribute a publication without government approval, and publishers must submit to ongoing government supervision.[138] To obtain government approval, a publisher must meet minimum capital requirements, obtain a government-approved sponsor, and accord with the state's own plans for the publishing industry.[139] Once approved, publishers must submit written reports of their publishing activities to the government and seek advance approval to publish on matters that involve "state security" or "social stability."[140] In March 2011, the State Council amended the Regulations of the Administration of Publications, leaving these general requirements intact and adding new provisions requiring those who distribute publications over the Internet or information networks to obtain a license and requiring specialized personnel to take a state exam to show compliance with state-imposed qualifications.[141]

Those who "illegally" engage in business activities, including publishing without a license, remain subject to criminal penalties under Article 225 of the PRC Criminal Law, and officials continue to use this charge to target political speech.[142] In August 2010, authorities in Shaanxi province detained author and journalist Xie Chaoping on this charge after he published a book on the relocation of citizens affected by a hydroelectric dam.[143] Prosecutors refused to approve Xie's arrest for insufficient evidence.[144] In December 2010, authorities took Mongol writer Erden-uul into custody in apparent connection to a new book he authored that reportedly addressed Inner Mongolian independence from China, saying the writer had engaged in "illegal publishing."[145] The Chinese government reported in September 2010 that Mongol rights advocate Sodmongol was being tried in connection to "counterfeiting book registration numbers and illegally publishing and selling books."[146] In April 2010 authorities detained Sodmongol while he was en route to attend the UN Permanent Forum on Indigenous Issues.[147]

Government agencies police content based on vague and sweeping prohibitions on content deemed by officials to "destroy ethnic unity, or infringe upon ethnic customs and habits," "propagate evil cults or superstition," or "harm the honor or interests of the nation."[148] Provincial and local authorities continued to target "illegal" political and religious publications. In March 2011, a Chinese news report said authorities in Heilongjiang province would "strictly confiscate political illegal publications and publications that defame the Party and state leaders, along with illegal publications that incite ethnic division."[149] It also said authorities would emphasize blocking and confiscating "illegal political publications" that "hostile foreign forces cook up," or that "domestic lawless persons illegally print or copy to disseminate political rumors," or that "create ideological confusion."[150] In April, authorities in Jiangxi province seized some 632 publications that constituted "illegal religious propaganda."[151] Also in April, authorities in Guang'an city, Sichuan province, reportedly destroyed some 30 items that were "illegal political publications, [related to the] Falun Gong cult organization, and illegal religious propaganda," as well as 1,141 "illegal newspapers and journals."[152]

Endnotes

[1] International Covenant on Civil and Political Rights, adopted by UN General Assembly resolution 2200A (XXI) of 16 December 66, entry into force 23 March 76, art. 19(3); Universal Declaration of Human Rights, adopted and proclaimed by UN General Assembly resolution 217A (III) of 10 December 48, arts. 19, 29. The UN Special Rapporteur on the Promotion and Protection of the Right to Freedom of Opinion and Expression has also used this three-factor test to describe the standard for determining when a restriction is permissible under Article 19, paragraph 3, of the ICCPR. UN Human Rights Council, Report of the Special Rapporteur on the Promotion and Protection of the Right to Freedom of Opinion and Expression, Frank La Rue, 16 May 11, A/HRC/17/27, para. 24.

[2] UN GAOR, Hum. Rts. Coun., 12th Sess., Promotion and Protection of All Human Rights, Civil, Political, Economic, Social and Cultural Rights, Including the Right to Development, adopted by Human Rights Council resolution 12/16, A/HRC/RES/12/16, 12 October 09, para. 5(p)(i).

[3] In its May 2011 report, the Special Rapporteur on the Promotion and Protection of the Right to Freedom of Opinion and Expression stated that "any legislation restricting the right to freedom of expression must be applied by a body which is independent of any political, commercial, or other unwarranted influences in a manner that is neither arbitrary nor discriminatory, and with adequate safeguards against abuse, including the possibility of challenge and remedy against its abusive application." UN Human Rights Council, Report of the Special Rapporteur on the Promotion and Protection of the Right to Freedom of Opinion and Expression, Frank La Rue, 16 May 11, A/HRC/17/27, para. 24.

[4] Wu Yu, "'Jasmine Revolution' Circulates Online, Chinese Authorities Take Precautions on All Fronts" [Wangchuan "molihua geming," zhongguo dangju quanxian jiebei], Deutsche Welle, 19 February 11.

[5] "China's 'Jasmine Revolution,' Assembly Sites in Each Major City" [Zhongguo "molihua geming" geda chengshi jihui didian], Boxun, 19 February 11; Wu Yu, "'Jasmine Revolution' Circulates Online, Chinese Authorities Take Precautions on All Fronts" [Wangchuan "molihua geming," zhongguo dangju quanxian jiebei], Deutsche Welle, 19 February 11; Human Rights in China, "Jasmine Organizers Call for Rallies Every Sunday," 22 February 11.

[6] "Latest Directives From the Ministry of Truth, January 2–28, 2011," China Digital Times, 8 February 11; "Latest Directives From the Ministry of Truth, February 17–24, 2011," China Digital Times, 23 February 11. For CECC analysis, see "Authorities Censor Access to Information on Middle East and Chinese 'Jasmine' Protests," Congressional-Executive Commission on China, 22 March 11.

[7] Jeremy Page, "Beijing Blocks Protest Reports," Wall Street Journal, 31 January 11; Edward Wong and David Barboza, "Wary of Egypt Unrest, China Censors Web," New York Times, 31 January 11. See, e.g., "Color Revolutions Will Not Bring About Real Democracy," Global Times, 30 January 11.

[8] Michael Kan, "China Microblogs Block Chinese Word for 'Egypt,'" IDG News, reprinted in PCWorld, 29 January 11; Jeremy Page, "China Co-Opts Social Media To Head Off Unrest," Wall Street Journal, 22 February 11. For CECC analysis, see "Authorities Censor Access to Information on Middle East and Chinese 'Jasmine' Protests," Congressional-Executive Commission on China, 22 March 11.

[9] Chinese Human Rights Defenders, "Escalating Crackdown Following Call for 'Jasmine Revolution' in China," 31 March 11. For CECC analysis, see "Authorities Crack Down on Rights Defenders, Lawyers, Artists, Bloggers," Congressional-Executive Commission on China, 3 May 11.

[10] Ibid.

[11] UN Office of the High Commissioner for Human Rights, "China: UN Expert Body Concerned About Recent Wave of Enforced Disappearances," 8 April 11; Human Rights Watch, "China: Arrests, Disappearances Require International Response," 31 March 11; Amnesty International, "China: New Generation of Internet Activists Targeted," 23 March 11.

[12] Barbara Demick, "China Has Many 'Dirty Words,'" Los Angeles Times, 21 April 10; Loretta Chao and Jason Dean, "China's Censors Thrive in Obscurity," Wall Street Journal, 31 March 10. Zhang Lei, "Publish and Be Deleted," Global Times, 25 February 10.

[13] Andrew Jacobs, "China, Angered by Peace Prize, Blocks Celebration," New York Times, 9 October 10; "PRC Blocks Web, Text Message Reports of Peace Prize for Liu Xiaobo," Agence France-Presse, 8 October 10; Pascale Trouillaud, "China Wages Propaganda War After Nobel," Agence France-Presse, reprinted in Google, 11 October 10.

[14] "New Controls on Text Messages," Radio Free Asia, 6 January 11.

[15] "China, Tibet: The End of TibetCul.com?" Global Voices, 19 March 11; "Graft-Busting Site Blocked," Radio Free Asia, 11 January 11; "China Closes AIDS Website," Radio Free Asia, 16 March 11.

[16] Sky Canaves, "What Are You Allowed To Say on China's Social Networks?" IEEE Spectrum, June 2011.

[17] Reporters Without Borders, "Internet Is Collateral Victim of Crackdown on Inner Mongolia Protests," 31 May 11. For CECC analysis, see "Mongols Protest in Inner Mongolia After Clashes Over Grasslands Use, Mining Operations," Congressional-Executive Commission on China, 1 July 11.

[18] Chinese Human Rights Defenders, "News Flash: Rights Defender Wang Yi About To Be Sent to Reeducation Through Labor" [Kuai xun: weiquan renshi wang yi zheng yao bei song qu laojiao], reprinted in Boxun, 15 November 10; Amnesty International, "Chinese Woman Sentenced to a Year in Labour Camp Over Tweet," 17 November 10. For CECC analysis, see "Henan Authorities Order One-Year Reeducation Through Labor Sentence for Activist's Satirical Tweet," CECC China Human Rights and Rule of Law Update, No. 9, 10 December 10, 3.

[19] Ibid.

[20] "Netizen 'Re-educated' for Online Rant," Radio Free Asia, 6 June 11.

[21] Didi Kirsten Tatlow, "Caught in an 'Authoritarian Moment,'" New York Times, 25 November 10.

[22] Chinese Human Rights Defenders, "A Quiet Crackdown, Yet Likely the Harshest in Recent Years," 25 February 11.

[23] "Guangzhou Lawyer Liu Zhengqing Arrested and House Searched, Zheng Chuangtian Seeks Defense and Hua Chunhui Receives Reeducation Through Labor" [Guangzhou lushi liu zhengqing beibu chaojia, zheng chuangtian qubao hua chunhui chuan laojiao], Radio Free Asia, 1 April 11.

[24] Chinese Human Rights Defenders, "A Quiet Crackdown, Yet Likely the Harshest in Recent Years," 25 February 11.

[25] Measures for the Administration of Internet Information Services [Hulianwang xinxi fuwu guanli banfa], issued 20 September 00, effective 25 September 00, art. 15.

[26] See, e.g., a November 2010 China Daily article that notes the concerns of one Chinese professor, who said there is a need for specific laws to determine when citizens have "spread rumors." Li Xinzhu, "Latest Batch of Rogue Netizens Exposed," China Daily, 3 November 10.

[27] Measures for the Administration of Internet Information Services [Hulianwang xinxi fuwu guanli banfa], issued 20 September 00, effective 25 September 00, arts. 15–16; Provisions on the Administration of Internet News Information Services [Hulianwang xinwen xinxi fuwu guanli guiding], issued 25 September 05, effective 25 September 05, arts. 19–21.

[28] Lana Lam, "Social Media Finding Ways Around Censors," South China Morning Post, 13 February 11.

[29] Zhang Duo, et al., "Online Media Visit 'First Congress' Meeting Site in Nanhu, Li Yanhong Speaks on Behalf of Members" [Wangluo meiti tanfang "yi da" huizhi nanhu li yanhong daibiao chengyuan fayan], Xinhua, 8 June 11.

[30] Melanie Lee, "Sina To Launch English Microblog by Year-End," Reuters, 7 June 11.

[31] Loretta Chao, "Google Objects to China's Acts," Wall Street Journal, 22 March 11.

[32] Chris Buckley, "Ministry Spokeswoman Says Accusations 'Unacceptable,'" Reuters, 22 March 11.

[33] "Ensuring Your Information Is Safe Online," The Official Google Blog, 1 June 11.

[34] Michael Wines, "China Rejects Google's Hacking Charge," New York Times, 6 June 11.

[35] Measures for the Administration of Internet Information Services [Hulianwang xinxi fuwu guanli banfa], issued 20 September 00, effective 25 September 00, art. 4; Registration Administration Measures for Non-Commercial Internet Information Services [Fei jingyingxing hulianwang xinxi fuwu bei'an guanli banfa], issued 28 January 05, effective 20 March 05, art. 5; Provisions on the Administration of Internet News Information Services [Hulianwang xinwen xinxi fuwu guanli guiding], issued 25 September 05, effective 25 September 05, arts. 5, 11, 12; Provisions on the Administration of Internet Video and Audio Programming Services [Hulianwang shiting jiemu fuwu guanli guiding], issued 20 December 07, effective 31 January 08, art. 7.

[36] The Special Rapporteur also noted that such licensing schemes should be distinguished from "registration with a domain name authority for purely technical reasons or rules of general application which apply without distinction to any kind of commercial operation." UN Human Rights Council, Report of the Special Rapporteur on the Promotion and Protection of the Right to Freedom of Opinion and Expression, Frank La Rue, 16 May 11, A/HRC/17/27, para. 28. In China, because the registration system gives the government discretion to reject an application based on content (i.e., whether the Web site operator intends to post "news," and if so, whether it is authorized to do so), it is qualitatively different from registration which all Web site operators must undertake with a domain registrar, and constitutes a de facto licensing scheme. Measures for the Administration of Internet Information Services [Hulianwang xinxi fuwu guanli banfa], issued 20 September 00, effective 25 September 00, art. 4; Registration Administration Measures for Non-Commercial Internet Information Services [Fei jingyingxing hulianwang xinxi fuwu bei'an guanli banfa], issued 28 January 05, effective 20 March 05, art. 5.

[37] "Nationwide 3000 Web Sites Closed for Failing To Register, 636,000 Domain Names No Longer Resolving" [Quanguo guanbi 3000 ge wei bei'an wangzhan, tingzhi jiexi 63.6 wan yuming], Sina, 28 October 10.

[38] Yin Yungong and Liu Ruisheng, "The Indigenization and Socialization of China's New Media—Characteristics, Dissemination Influence, and Hot Topic Analysis in the Development of New Media in China in 2010" [Zhongguo xin meiti de bentuhua yu shehuihua—2010 nian zhongguo xin meiti fazhan tezheng, chuanbo yingxiang yu redian jiexi], taken from the Chinese New Media Development Report (2011) [Zhongguo xin meiti fazhan baogao (2011)], Chinese Academy of Social Sciences, Media and Communications Research Web, 12 July 11.

[39] Priscilla Jiao, "41pc of Mainland Websites Close in Just One Year," South China Morning Post, 13 July 11.

[40] Ibid.

[41] Yin Yungong and Liu Ruisheng, "The Indigenization and Socialization of China's New Media—Characteristics, Dissemination Influence, and Hot Topic Analysis in the Development of New Media in China in 2010" [Zhongguo xin meiti de bentuhua yu shehuihua—2010 nian zhongguo xin meiti fazhan tezheng, chuanbo yingxiang yu redian jiexi], taken from the Chinese New Media Development Report (2011) [Zhongguo xin meiti fazhan baogao (2011)], Chinese Academy of Social Sciences, Media and Communications Research Web, 12 July 11.

[42] State Council Information Office, "White Paper on the State of the Internet in China" [Zhongguo hulianwang zhuangkuang bai pi shu], 8 June 10, sec. I.

[43] China Internet Network Information Center, "27th Statistical Report on Internet Development in China" [Di 27 ci zhongguo hulianwangluo fazhan zhuangkuang diaocha tongji baogao], 19 January 11, 12, 21; Ministry of Industry and Information Technology, "Ministry of Industry and Information Technology Announces April 2011 Telecommunications Industry Operating Sit-

uation" [Gongye he xinxihua bu fabu 2011 nian 4 yue tongxinye yunxing zhuangkuang], 24 May 11.

[44] "Wang Chen: Chinese Government Attaches Great Importance to and Actively Promotes the Development and Utilization of the Internet" [Wang chen: zhongguo zhengfu gaodu zhongshi bing jiji cujin hulianwang fazhan yu yunyong], China.com, 30 December 10; "Hu Jintao: Firmly Raise the Standard for Scientization of Social Management" [Hu jintao: zhazhashishi tigao shehui guanli kexuehua shuiping], Xinhua, 19 February 11.

[45] Guobin Yang, "China's Gradual Revolution," New York Times, 13 March 11; Keith B. Richburg, "In China, Microblogging Sites Become Free-Speech Platform," Washington Post, 27 March 11; Michael Wines, "China's Censors Misfire in Abuse-of-Power Case," New York Times, 17 November 10. One U.S.-based Chinese Internet expert tallied 60 major cases of online activism in 2009 and 2010, but noted that the protests were primarily local and directed at corrupt officials and specific instances of injustice and that government controls had prevented more "broad-based coalitions." Guobin Yang, "China's Gradual Revolution," New York Times, 13 March 11.

[46] Michael Wines and Sharon LaFraniere, "In Baring Facts of Train Crash, Blogs Erode China Censorship," New York Times, 28 July 11.

[47] Ibid.

[48] "State Internet Information Office Established" [Guojia hulianwang xinxi bangongshi sheli], Xinhua, reprinted in State Council Information Office, 4 May 11.

[49] In an April 2011 Chinese news article, an official with the Beijing City Internet Propaganda Supervision Office noted that the "basic principle of the Communist Party managing the media" had been legally enshrined in major Internet regulations and that the government body in charge of managing the media, the State Council Information Office, and the Central Party External Propaganda Office were simply "the same office under different names." Chen Hua, "Looking Back on Ten Years of Internet News Publishing Work and the Avenues of Management by Law" [Hulianwang zhan dengzai xinwen yewu shinian huigu yu fazhi guanli lujing], Qianlong Net, 29 April 11.

[50] "Hu Jintao: Firmly Raise the Standard for Scientization of Social Management" [Hu jintao: zhazhashishi tigao shehui guanli kexuehua shuiping], Xinhua, 19 February 11.

[51] Pascale Trouillaud, "China's Web Spin Doctors Spread Beijing's Message," Sydney Morning Herald, 12 May 11.

[52] "Zhou Yongkang: Adapt to New Economic and Social Development Conditions, Strengthen and Create Innovations in Social Management" [Zhou yongkang: shiying jingji shehui fazhan xin xingshi, jiaqiang he chuangxin shehui guanli], Xinhua, 20 February 11.

[53] Andrew Jacobs, "As China Steps Up Web Monitoring, Many Wi-Fi Users Stay Away," New York Times, 25 July 11; Xu Tianran, "Is Wi-Fi Software Illegal?" Global Times, 29 July 11.

[54] Dui Hua Foundation, "Official Data Show State Security Arrests, Prosecutions Remained at Historic Levels in 2010," 15 March 11. Article 105 provides for sentences of up to life imprisonment for attempts to subvert state power or up to 15 years for inciting such subversion. PRC Criminal Law, enacted 1 July 79, amended 14 March 97, effective 1 October 97, amended 25 December 99, 31 August 01, 29 December 01, 28 December 02, 28 February 05, 29 June 06, 28 February 09, art. 105.

[55] Chinese Human Rights Defenders, "Individuals Affected by the Crackdown Following Call for 'Jasmine Revolution,'" updated 30 May 11.

[56] Ibid.

[57] Andrew Jacobs, "China Releases Dissident Blogger, With Conditions," New York Times, 10 August 11.

[58] Chinese Human Rights Defenders, "Escalating Crackdown Following Call for 'Jasmine Revolution' in China," 31 March 11.

[59] PRC Criminal Law, enacted 1 July 79, amended 14 March 97, effective 1 October 97, amended 25 December 99, 31 August 01, 29 December 01, 28 December 02, 28 February 05, 29 June 06, 28 February 09, art. 293.

[60] Chinese Human Rights Defenders, "Individuals Affected by the Crackdown Following Call for 'Jasmine Revolution,'" updated 30 May 11.

[61] "Chinese Activist on Trial Amid Crackdowns," Associated Press, reprinted in Time, 11 August 11.

[62] Tania Branigan, "Chinese Internet Activist Wang Lihong Goes on Trial," Guardian, 12 August 11.

[63] Human Rights in China, "Lawyers Report Procedural Irregularities at Trial of Rights Activist Wang Lihong," 13 August 11.

[64] Human Rights in China, "Rights Defender Wang Lihong Sentenced to Nine Months," 9 September 11.

[65] "Ai Weiwei's Company Evades 'Huge Amount' of Tax: Police," Xinhua, 20 May 11.

[66] Andrew Jacobs, "China Takes Dissident Artist Into Custody," New York Times, 3 April 11.

[67] "Wife of Detained Chinese Artist Finds Him Tense During Visit; No Word on Why He Was Seized," Associated Press, 15 May 11.

[68] Jeremy Page, "Ai Weiwei Resumes His Defiance of Beijing," Wall Street Journal, 12 August 11.

[69] Ibid.

[70] Ibid.

[71] Chinese Human Rights Defenders, "Individuals Affected by the Crackdown Following Call for 'Jasmine Revolution,'" updated 30 May 11.

[72] Following its 2005 visit to China, the UN Working Group on Arbitrary Detention noted that the vague definition of crimes of endangering national security, splitting the state, subverting state power, and supplying state secrets "leaves their application open to abuse particularly of the rights to freedom of religion, speech, and assembly." It recommended that political crimes "that leave large discretion to law enforcement and prosecution authorities such as 'endangering

national security,' 'subverting State power,' 'undermining the unity of the country,' 'supplying of State secrets to individuals abroad,' etc. should be abolished." Manfred Nowak, Report of the Special Rapporteur on Torture and Other Cruel, Inhuman or Degrading Treatment or Punishment, Mission to China, 10 March 06, paras. 34, 82(s). In a January 2008 report, Chinese Human Rights Defenders studied 41 cases from 2000 to 2007 in which officials used the "inciting subversion" provision of the PRC Criminal Law (Article 105(2)) to punish Chinese citizens for exercising their right to freedom of expression. It found that in such cases "[t]he 'evidence' often consists of no more than the writings of an individual or simply shows that he/she circulated certain articles containing dissenting views, without any effort to show that the expression had any potential or real subversive effect. That is to say, speech in and of itself is interpreted as constituting incitement of subversion. . . ." Chinese Human Rights Defenders, "Inciting Subversion of State Power: A Legal Tool for Prosecuting Free Speech in China," 8 January 08. See, e.g., a Beijing court's December 2009 decision in the Liu Xiaobo case in which the court provided no evidence that Liu advocated violence in his works. Human Rights in China, "Case Update: International Community Speaks Out on Liu Xiaobo Verdict," 30 December 09. For CECC analysis, see "Liu Xiaobo Appeals Sentence; Official Abuses Mar Case From Outset," CECC China Human Rights and Rule of Law Update, No. 2, 5 February 10, 2.

[73] Chinese Human Rights Defenders, "Wuhan Rights Defender Li Tie Arrested on Suspicion of 'Subverting State Power' Crime" [Wuhan weiquan renshi litie bei yi shexian "dianfu guojia zhengquan zui" daibu], 17 November 10.

[74] "Chinese Activist Held Over Tiananmen Picture," Associated Press, reprinted in Guardian, 30 November 10.

[75] International Campaign for Tibet, "Three More Tibetan Writers Sentenced to Prison," 21 January 11; "Tibetan Writers Sentenced," Radio Free Asia, 31 December 10; International Campaign for Tibet, "Three Tibetan Writers on Trial Await Verdict," 5 November 10; "Tibetan Writers Tried as 'Splittists,'" Radio Free Asia, 5 November 10.

[76] Human Rights in China, "Activist Sentenced to Ten Years for Inciting Subversion; Essays Cited as Evidence," 25 March 11.

[77] "So-Called 'Punishment Because of Speech' Is a Misreading of the Judgment in the Liu Xiaobo Case" [Suowei "yinyan huozui" shi dui liu xiaobo an panjue de wudu], Xinhua, 25 October 10. For CECC analysis, see "Xinhua Article Claims Liu Xiaobo Case Meets International Standards," CECC China Human Rights and Rule of Law Update, No. 9, 10 December 10, 1–2.

[78] Ibid.

[79] Ibid.

[80] UN Working Group on Arbitrary Detention, Opinion No. 15/2011 (People's Republic of China), 5 May 11, reprinted in Freedom Now, 1 August 11. For CECC analysis, see "UN Group Calls for Immediate Release of Liu Xiaobo and Wife Liu Xia," Congressional-Executive Commission on China, 12 August 11.

[81] Reporters Without Borders, "Debate on Internet Censorship Censored," 30 November 10; "Guizhou Poet 'Still Missing,'" Radio Free Asia, 16 December 10.

[82] ChinaAid, "Urgent! Chen and Wife Beaten Severely, Chinese Citizens Appeal to America," 10 February 11; China Human Rights Lawyers Concern Group, "Vehemently Condemn Beating and Taking Into Custody Rights Defense Lawyer" [Qianglie qianze ouda ji jujin weiquan lushi], 21 February 11. For CECC analysis, see "Chen Guangcheng, Wife Reportedly Beaten After Release of Video Detailing Official Abuse," Congressional-Executive Commission on China, 11 March 11.

[83] Ibid.

[84] PEN American Center, "PEN Sounds Alarm Over Treatment of Jailed Nobel Laureate's Wife in China," 22 February 11.

[85] UN Working Group on Arbitrary Detention, Opinion No. 15/2011 (People's Republic of China), 5 May 11, reprinted in Freedom Now, 1 August 11. For CECC analysis, see "UN Group Calls for Immediate Release of Liu Xiaobo and Wife Liu Xia," Congressional-Executive Commission on China, 12 August 11.

[86] Chinese Human Rights Defenders, "Qin Yongmin, Recently Released From Prison, Suffers High Blood Pressure After Being Abused by Police During Visit" [Gang chuyu de qin yongmin yin jingcha shangmen manma, zhi xueya dou sheng chuxian yanzhong bushi], 1 December 10.

[87] Philip Gourevitch, "Liao Yiwu: Grounded in China," New Yorker, 30 March 11; "China Bans Writer From Traveling Abroad," Associated Press, 9 May 11. Earlier, officials had allowed Liao to attend a literary festival in Germany in September 2010.

[88] Didi Kirsten Tatlow, "Chinese Artists Drawn to Berlin, a Haven That Reveres History," New York Times, 10 August 11.

[89] Human Rights in China, "Three Documents Related to the Case of Buddhist Leader Wu Zeheng," 22 September 11.

[90] Ibid.

[91] UN Human Rights Council, "Tenth Anniversary Joint Declaration: Ten Key Challenges to Freedom of Expression in the Next Decade," Addendum to Report of the Special Rapporteur on the Promotion and Protection of the Rights to Freedom of Opinion and Expression, Frank La Rue, 25 March 10, A/HRC/14/23/Add.2, art. 1(a).

[92] "Liu Binjie: Political System Reform Must Insist on the Correct Orientation" [Liu binjie: zhengzhi tizhi gaige bixu jianchi zhengque fangxiang], China Press and Publications Daily, 17 November 10.

[93] "SARFT Spokesperson: Radio and Televisions Not Allowed To Entirely Go on Market" [Guangdian zongju xinwen fayan ren: diantai dianshitai buxu zhengti shangshi], China News Net, 14 January 11.

[94] Zhao Qiang, "Loss of Control Over Public Opinion: Catalyst for Disintegration of Soviet Union" [Yulun shikong: sulian jieti de cuihuaji], Seeking Truth, 1 November 10.

[95] "Local Newspapers Prohibited From Swapping Reports, Freedom of Speech in the Mainland Again Put Under Pressure" [Difang baozhang jin huhuan gaojian neidi yanlunziyou zai yu ya], Ming Pao, 15 July 10; Reporters Without Borders, "New Regulations Pose Threat to Liberal Press," 21 July 10. For CECC analysis, see "Communist Party Seeks To Restrict Already Limited Critical Media Reports," CECC China Human Rights and Rule of Law Update, No. 8, 9 November 10, 4.

[96] "Does China's General Administration on Press and Publication Safeguard or Restrict Freedom of the Press?" [Zhongguo xinwen chuban shu weihu hai shi xianzhi xinwen ziyou?], Radio Free Asia, 6 November 10.

[97] Katherine Hille, "Anger Over Attacks on Journalists in China," Financial Times, 8 August 10.

[98] Ibid.

[99] Sharon LaFraniere, "Media Blackout in China After Wreck," New York Times, 31 July 11.

[100] Ibid.

[101] Ibid.

[102] "Remarks at 11th China Journalists' Day and Presentation of Awards and Report Meeting" [Zai di shiyi jie zhongguo jizhe jie ji banjiang baogao hui shang de jianghua], People's Daily, 8 November 10.

[103] Ibid.

[104] "Liu Yunshan Presides Over Convening of Meeting on Topic of Starting Propaganda Reporting Work for 90th Anniversary of the Party's Founding" [Liu yunshan zhuchi zhaokai jiandang 90 zhounian xuanchuan baodao gongzuo zhuanti huiyi], Xinhua, 22 April 11. For CECC analysis, see "Top Official Directs Media To Promote July Anniversary of Party's Founding," Congressional-Executive Commission on China, 1 July 11.

[105] Ibid.

[106] Damian Grammaticas, "Chinese Regulators Suspend TV Crime and Spy Dramas," BBC, 6 May 11.

[107] Keith Richburg, "Chinese Editors, and a Web Site, Detail Censors' Hidden Hand," Washington Post, 1 April 11.

[108] International Federation of Journalists, "New IFJ Report Outlines Restrictions on Journalists in China in 2010," 30 January 11.

[109] Ibid.

[110] Pascale Trouillaud, "China Wages Propaganda War After Nobel," Agence France-Presse, reprinted in Google, 11 October 10.

[111] Ibid.

[112] Wu Yu, "Chinese Authorities Issue Media Restriction, Banning 'Civil Society'" [Zhongguo dangju xiada meiti jinling, pingbi "gongmin shehui"], Deutsche Welle, 6 January 11.

[113] Priscilla Jiao, "Officials Put an End to Reporting Awards," South China Morning Post, 28 December 10.

[114] David Barboza, "Chinese Journalist Who Defied the Censors and Wrote About Corruption Is Fired," New York Times, 27 January 11.

[115] "'Time Weekly' Selection Crisis, Commentary Department Head 'Forced To Resign'" ["Shidai zhoubao" pingxuan fengbo, pinglunbu zhuren "bei cizhi"], Radio Free Asia, 10 January 11.

[116] Ibid.

[117] Ibid.

[118] Committee to Protect Journalists, "Mainstream Journalists Also Targeted in China Crackdown," 30 March 11.

[119] Priscilla Jiao, "High Price for Airing Sun Yat-sen Criticism," South China Morning Post, 19 August 11.

[120] International Federation of Journalists, "IFJ Demands Reinstatement of Journalist Suspended Over China Disaster Reports," 2 August 11.

[121] Provisions on the Administration of Internet News Information Services [Hulianwang xinwen xinxi fuwu guanli guiding], issued 25 September 05, effective 25 September 05, arts. 7, 8, 11; Regulations on the Administration of Publishing [Chuban guanli tiaoli], issued 25 December 01, effective 1 February 02, art. 15; Measures for Administration of News Reporter Cards [Xinwen jizhe zheng guanli banfa], issued 24 August 09, effective 15 October 09, arts. 11, 12, 16.

[122] Zhejiang Province Radio, Film and Television Bureau, "2010 Nationwide Radio and Television Editors and Reporters, Broadcasters, and Hosts Qualification Exam" [2010 nian quanguo guangbo dianshi bianji jizhe, boyin yuan zhuchi ren zige kaoshi dagang], 30 July 10, chap. 2, art. 6.

[123] CECC, 2010 Annual Report, 10 October 10, 68.

[124] "Stop False Reporting, Strengthen Social Responsibility, Strengthen Construction of News Professional Ethics" [Dujue xujia baodao, zengqiang shehui zeren, jiaqiang xinwen zhiye daode jianshe], Xinhua, 24 November 10.

[125] Ibid.

[126] "14 News Units Conscientiously Launch Self-Education and Self-Examination, Self-Rectification" [Shisi jia xinwen danwei renzhen kaizhan ziwo jiaoyu he zicha zijiu], Xinhua, 13 April 11.

[127] "Individual journalists should not be required to be licensed or to register. There should be no legal restrictions on who may practice journalism." UN Special Rapporteur on Freedom of Opinion and Expression, the Organization for Security and Cooperation in Europe Representative on Freedom of the Media, and the Organization of American States Special Rapporteur on Freedom of Expression, "International Experts Condemn Curbs on Freedom of Expression and Control Over Media and Journalists," UN Press Release, 18 December 03.

[128] UN Human Rights Council, "Tenth Anniversary Joint Declaration: Ten Key Challenges to Freedom of Expression in the Next Decade," Addendum to Report of the Special Rapporteur on

the Promotion and Protection of the Rights to Freedom of Opinion and Expression, Frank La Rue, 25 March 10, A/HRC/14/23/Add.2, arts. 1(b), 1(g).

[129] "GAPP's Special Campaign Against Newspaper and Magazine Journalist Stations" [Xinwen chuban zongshu jiang dui baokan jizhe zhan kaizhan zhuanxiang zhili], Xinhua, 24 March 11.

[130] Foreign Correspondents' Club of China, "Warning: Reporting on Chen Guangcheng," 17 February 11. For CECC analysis, see "Chen Guangcheng, Wife Reportedly Beaten After Release of Video Detailing Official Abuse," Congressional-Executive Commission on China, 11 March 11.

[131] Ibid.

[132] Foreign Correspondents' Club of China, "New Details on Wangfujing Interference," 28 February 11. For CECC analysis, see "Authorities Reportedly Beat, Detain, and Threaten Foreign Journalists Covering 'Jasmine Revolution,'" Congressional-Executive Commission on China, 22 March 11.

[133] Foreign Correspondents' Club of China, "New Details on Wangfujing Interference," 28 February 11; "Bloomberg Journalist Assaulted as China Heightens Security," Bloomberg, 27 February 11. For CECC analysis, see "Authorities Reportedly Beat, Detain, and Threaten Foreign Journalists Covering 'Jasmine Revolution,'" Congressional-Executive Commission on China, 22 March 11.

[134] "Foreign Minister to Foreign Press: Don't Believe Your Lying Eyes," Wall Street Journal, 8 March 11; Ministry of Foreign Affairs, "Foreign Ministry Spokesperson Jiang Yu's Regular Press Conference on March 3, 2011," 5 March 11. The Commission and others reported on the existence of local regulations issued in late 2010 and early 2011 that require official approval to report in the Wangfujing area and near the designated Shanghai protest site. For CECC analysis, see "Authorities Reportedly Beat, Detain, and Threaten Foreign Journalists Covering 'Jasmine Revolution,'" Congressional-Executive Commission on China, 22 March 11. But national regulations put in place for the 2008 Beijing Olympics provide that foreign journalists may interview any individual or organization so long as they obtain their consent. At the time, officials touted the regulations as providing foreign journalists freedom to report on every aspect of Chinese society, from political matters to social issues. Regulations of the People's Republic of China on News Covering Activities of the Permanent Offices of Foreign News Agencies and Foreign Journalists [Zhonghua renmin gongheguo waiguo changzhu xinwen jigou he waiguo jizhe caifang tiaoli], issued 17 October 08, art. 17; Ministry of Foreign Affairs, "Foreign Ministry News Department Head Liu Jianchao Hosts Sino-Foreign Journalists Press Conference on State Council's Promulgation of the 'Regulations of the People's Republic of China on News Covering Activities of the Permanent Offices of Foreign News Agencies and Foreign Journalists'" [Waijiaobu xinwen si sizhang liu jianchao jiu guowuyuan banbu shishi "zhonghua renmin gongheguo waiguo changzhu xinwen jigou he waiguo jizhe caifang tiaoli" juxing zhongwai jizhe hui], 17 October 08.

[135] Sharon LaFraniere and Edward Wong, "Even With Protests Averted, China Turns to Intimidation of Foreign Journalists," New York Times, 6 March 11; Alexa Olesen, "China Warns Foreign Media Not To Cover Protests," Associated Press, reprinted in Washington Post, 3 March 11.

[136] Louisa Lim, "China Cracks Down on Christians at Outdoor Service," National Public Radio, 11 April 11; Bill Schiller, "Star Reporter Detained, Interrogated by Chinese Police for Taking Photo," Toronto Star, 11 April 11.

[137] Ben Blanchard and Chris Buckley, "Foreign Media in China Face Worsening Conditions—Survey," Reuters, 19 May 11.

[138] Regulations on the Administration of Publishing [Chuban guanli tiaoli], issued 25 December 01, effective 1 February 02, amended 19 March 11, arts. 6, 7, 61; Provisions on the Administration of Newspaper Publishing [Baozhi chuban guanli guiding], issued 30 September 05, effective 1 December 05, arts. 2, 4; Provisions on the Administration of Periodical Publishing [Qikan chuban guanli guiding], issued 30 September 05, effective 1 December 05, arts. 2, 5.

[139] Regulations on the Administration of Publishing [Chuban guanli tiaoli], issued 25 December 01, effective 1 February 02, amended 19 March 11, art. 11.

[140] Provisions on the Administration of Periodical Publishing [Qikan chuban guanli guiding], issued 30 September 05, effective 1 December 05, art. 45 (written reports); Regulations on the Administration of Publishing [Chuban guanli tiaoli], issued 25 December 01, effective 1 February 02, amended 19 March 11, art. 20 (advance approval for special topics).

[141] Regulations on the Administration of Publishing [Chuban guanli tiaoli], issued 25 December 01, effective 1 February 02, amended 19 March 11, arts. 36, 53.

[142] PRC Criminal Law, enacted 1 July 79, amended 14 March 97, effective 1 October 97, amended 25 December 99, 31 August 01, 29 December 01, 28 December 02, 28 February 05, 29 June 06, 28 February 09, art. 225.

[143] "Procuratorate Decides Not To Arrest Author Xie Chaoping in Sanmenxia Dam Relocation Program 'Book Case,'" Congressional-Executive Commission on China, 10 December 10.

[144] Ibid.

[145] "Inner Mongolia Writer Unaga Secretly Detained for Publishing New Book" [Neimeng zuojia wunaga ni chuban xinshu zao mimi daibu], Radio Free Asia, 19 January 11; "Mongol Writer Unaga Secretly Arrested in Inner Mongolia" [Mongghul yazghuchisi unaga ichki mongghulda mexpiy tutuldi], Radio Free Asia, 18 January 11; Southern Mongolian Human Rights Information Center, "Southern Mongolian Dissident Writer, Author of 'Forefront of Independence' Arrested and Detained," 23 January 11.

[146] UN Human Rights Council, "Cases Examined by the Special Rapporteur (June 2009–July 2010)," Report of the Special Rapporteur on the Rights of Indigenous People, James Anaya, 15 September 10, A/HRC/15/37/Add.1.

[147] Ibid.

[148] Regulations on the Administration of Publishing [Chuban guanli tiaoli], issued 25 December 01, effective 1 February 02, amended 19 March 11, art. 25.

[149] "Strongly Rectify and Standardize Culture Market Order" [Zhongquan zhengdun guifan wenhua shichang zhixu], Heilongjiang Information Net, 11 March 11.

[150] Ibid.

[151] "Jiangxi Province 'Sweep Away Pornography and Strike Down Illegal Publications' Publications Market Program Clean-Up Has Remarkable Results" [Jiangxi sheng "saohuang dafei" chubanwu shichang zhuanxiang zhengzhi chengxiao xianzhu], People's Daily, 21 April 11.

[152] Liu Xilin, "Our City Has Destroyed More Than 60,000 Items of Rights—Violating, Pirated, and All Types of Illegal Publication" [Wo shi jizhong xiaohui 6 wan yu jian qinquan daoban ji gelei feifa chubanwu], Guang'an City Radio and Television Station, 22 April 11.

○

www.ingramcontent.com/pod-product-compliance
Lightning Source LLC
Chambersburg PA
CBHW082206290526

45794CB00008B/3449